AF375223

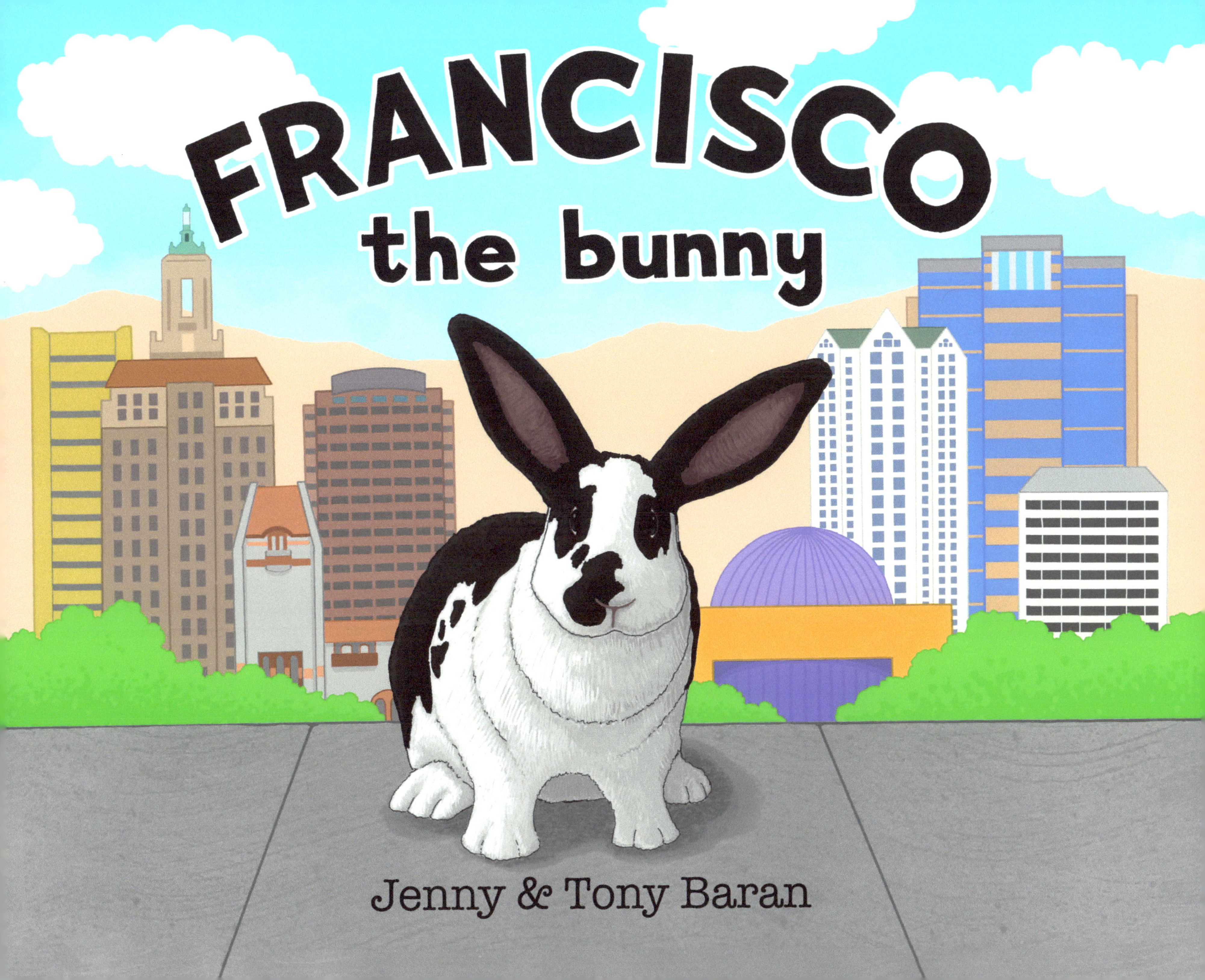

FRANCISCO
the bunny
Jenny & Tony Baran

Francisco the bunny

Written by: Jenny Baran
Illustrated by: Tony Baran

© Copyright 2022 Jenny & Tony Baran, Baran Family Arts

Digital ISBN: 979-8-9873990-5-7
Paperback ISBN: 979-8-9873990-8-8
Hard cover ISBN: 979-8-9873990-2-6

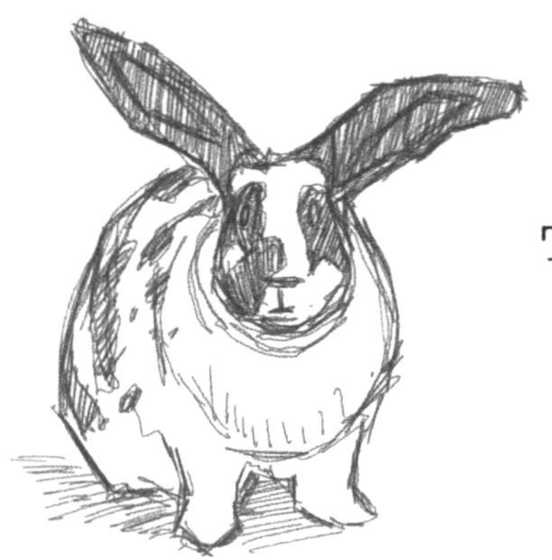

DEDICATION
To our children, Trevor and Angelica.
Be determined and hop, hop, hop!
Matthew 6:25-34
Love, Mommy & Daddy

This book belongs to:

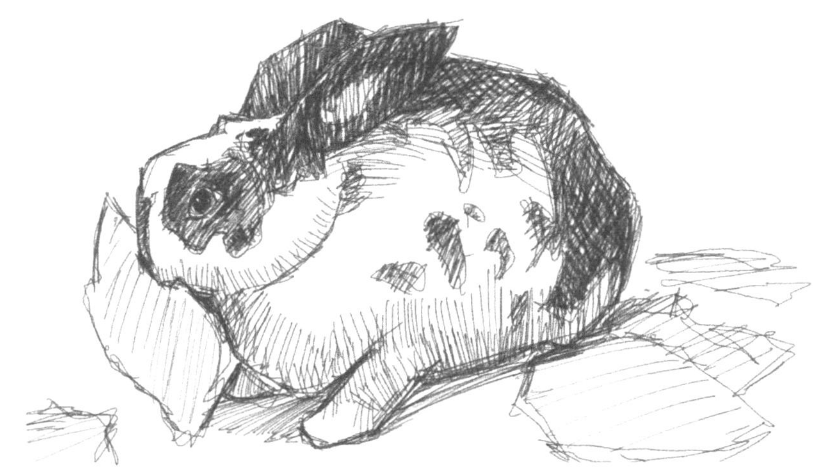

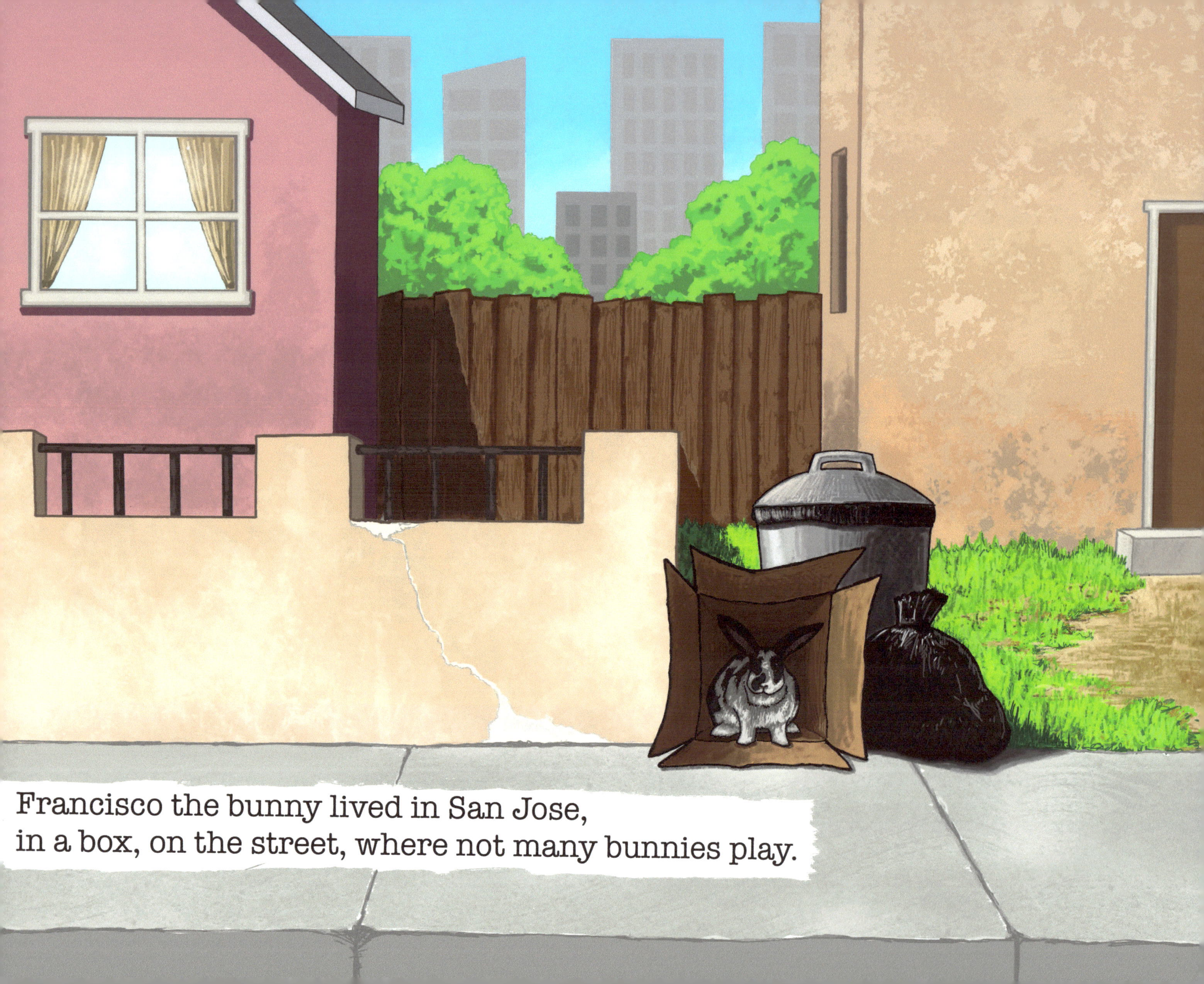

Francisco the bunny lived in San Jose,
in a box, on the street, where not many bunnies play.

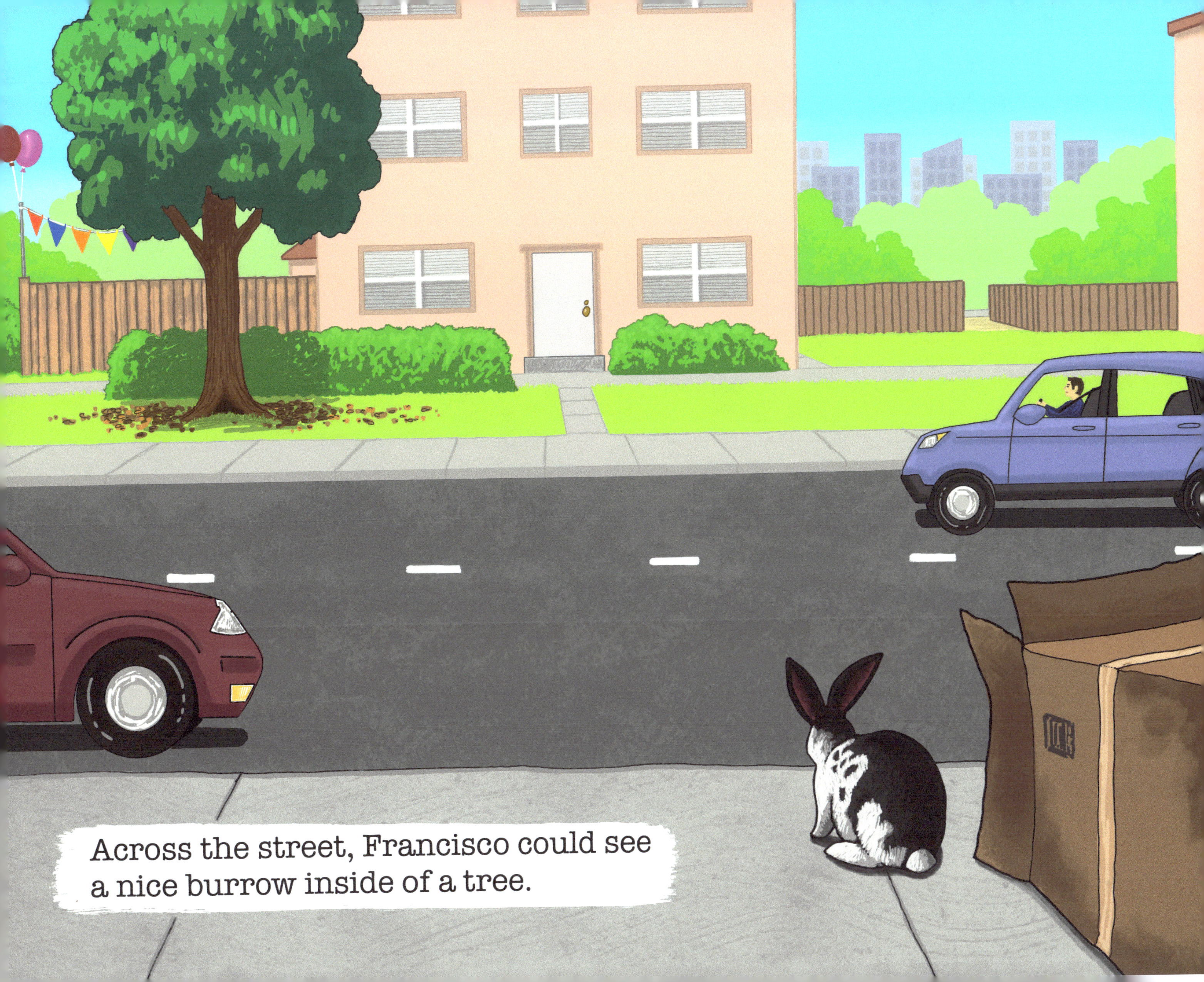
Across the street, Francisco could see a nice burrow inside of a tree.

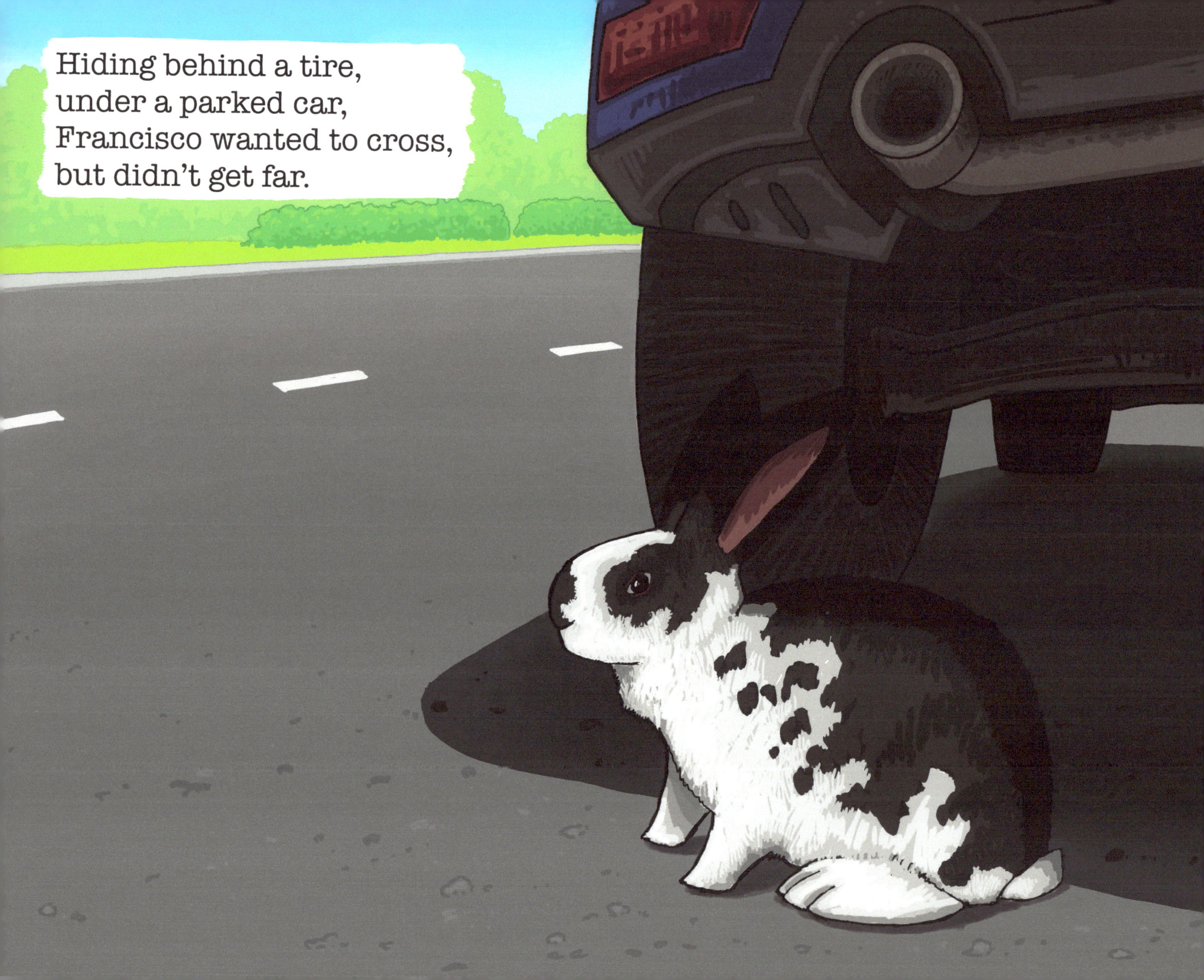

Hiding behind a tire,
under a parked car,
Francisco wanted to cross,
but didn't get far.

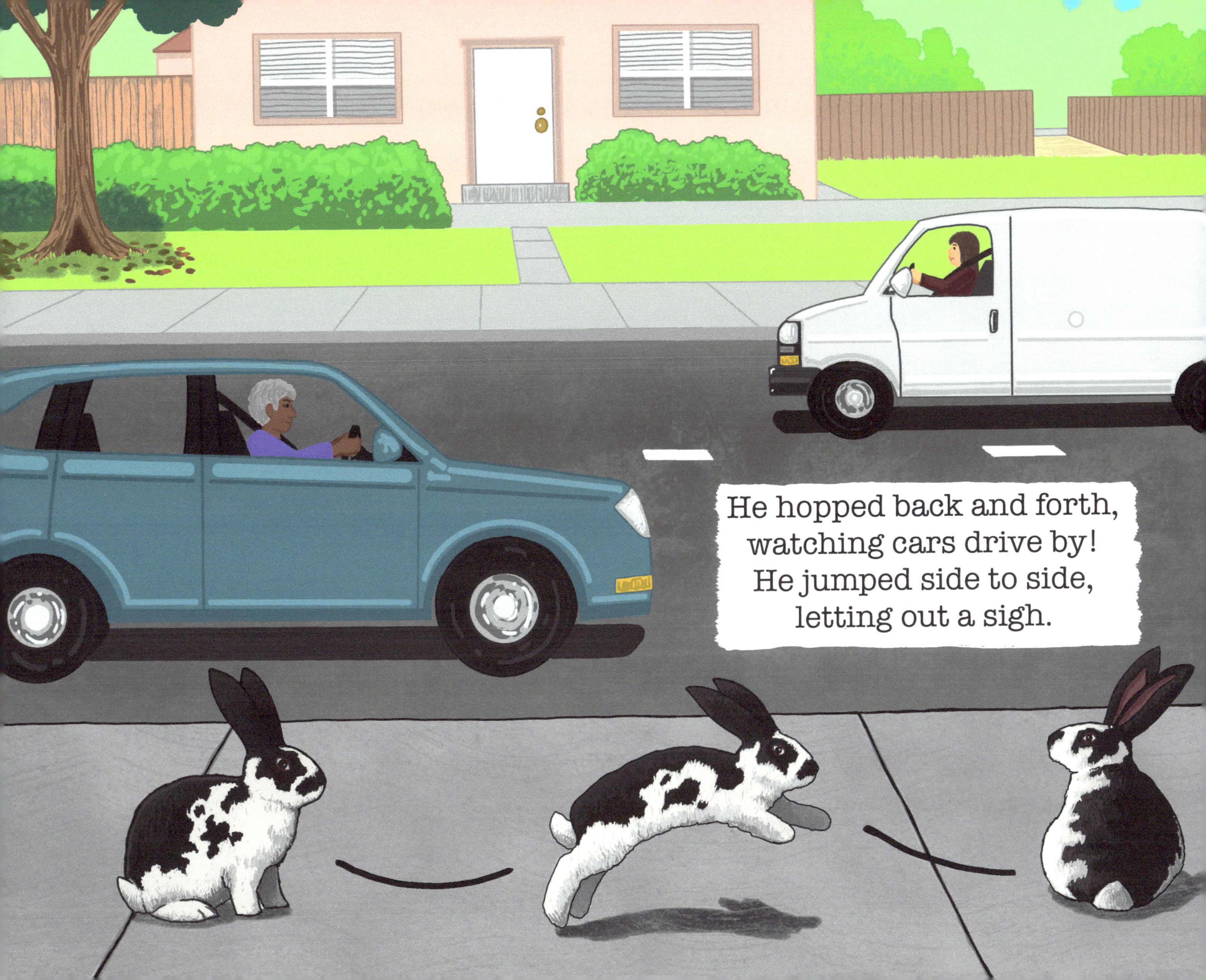

He hopped back and forth,
watching cars drive by!
He jumped side to side,
letting out a sigh.

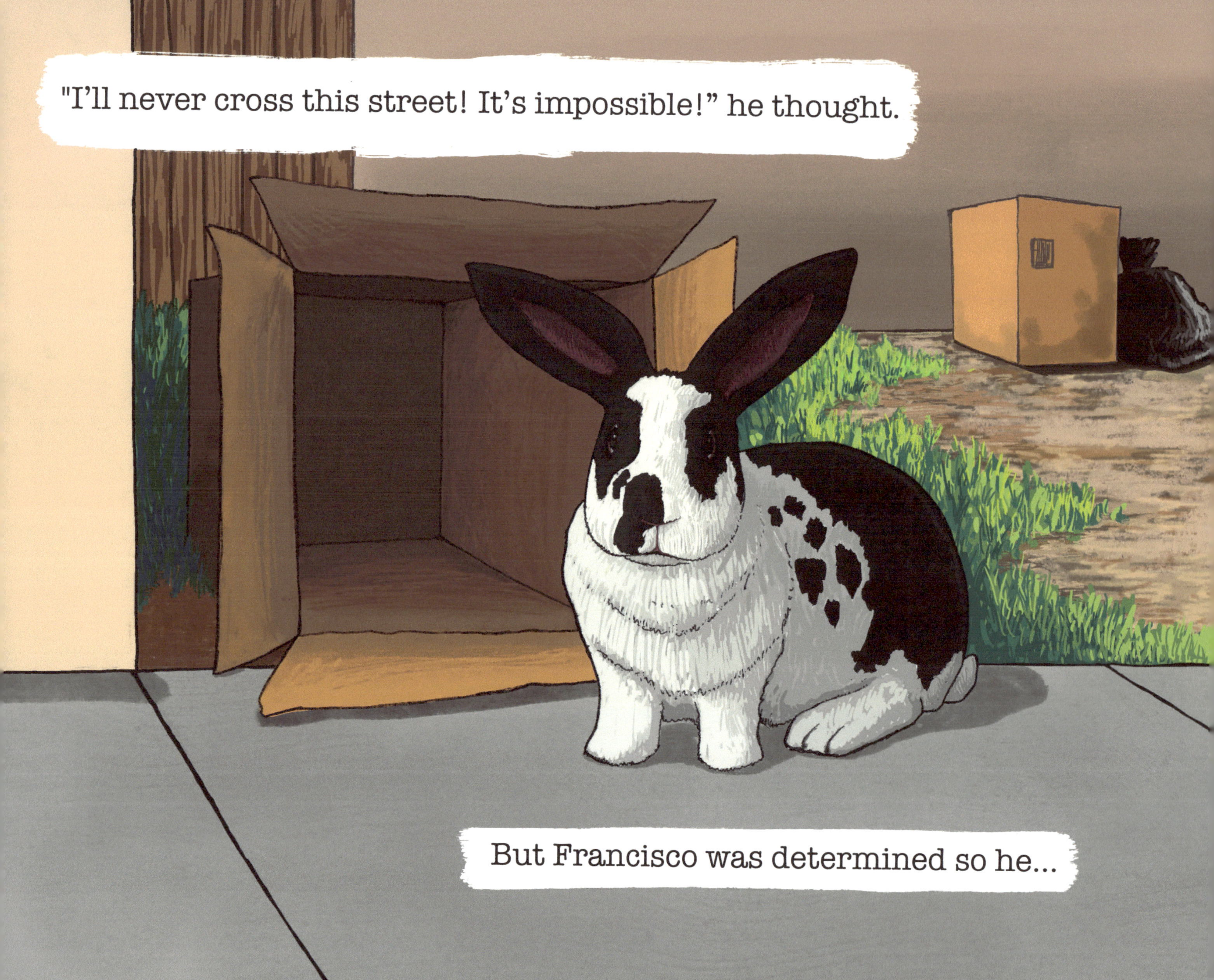

"I'll never cross this street! It's impossible!" he thought.
But Francisco was determined so he...

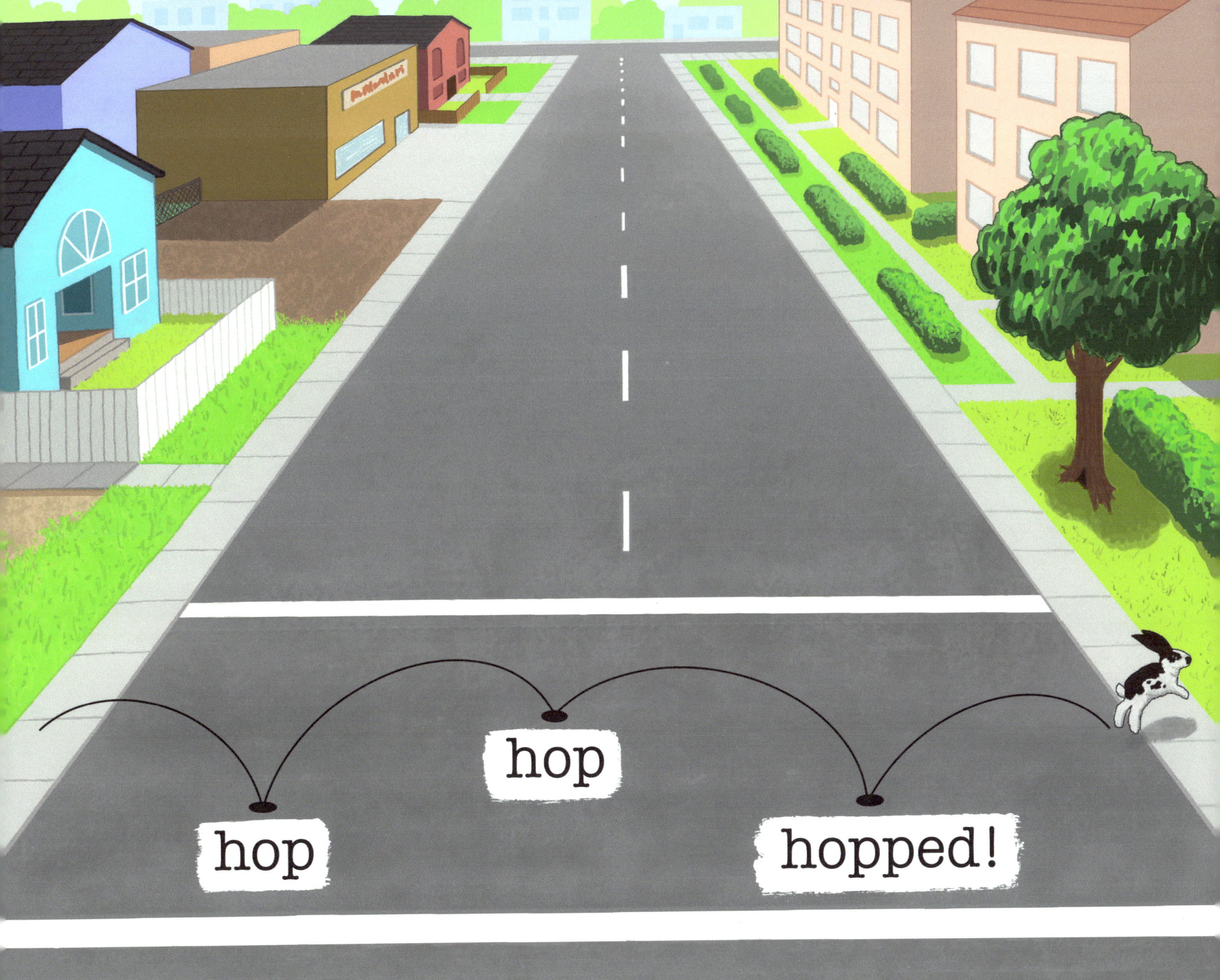

hop
hop
hopped!

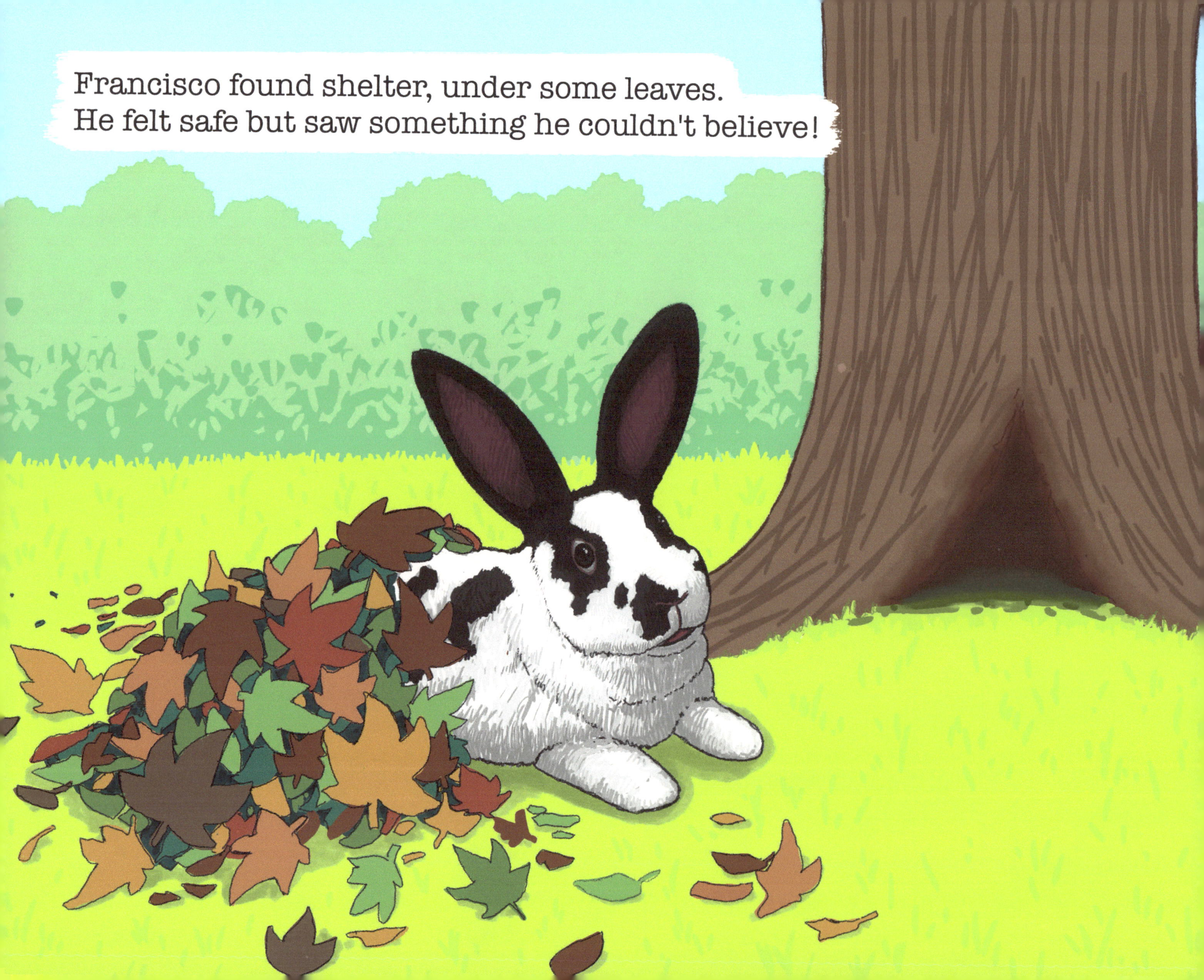
Francisco found shelter, under some leaves.
He felt safe but saw something he couldn't believe!

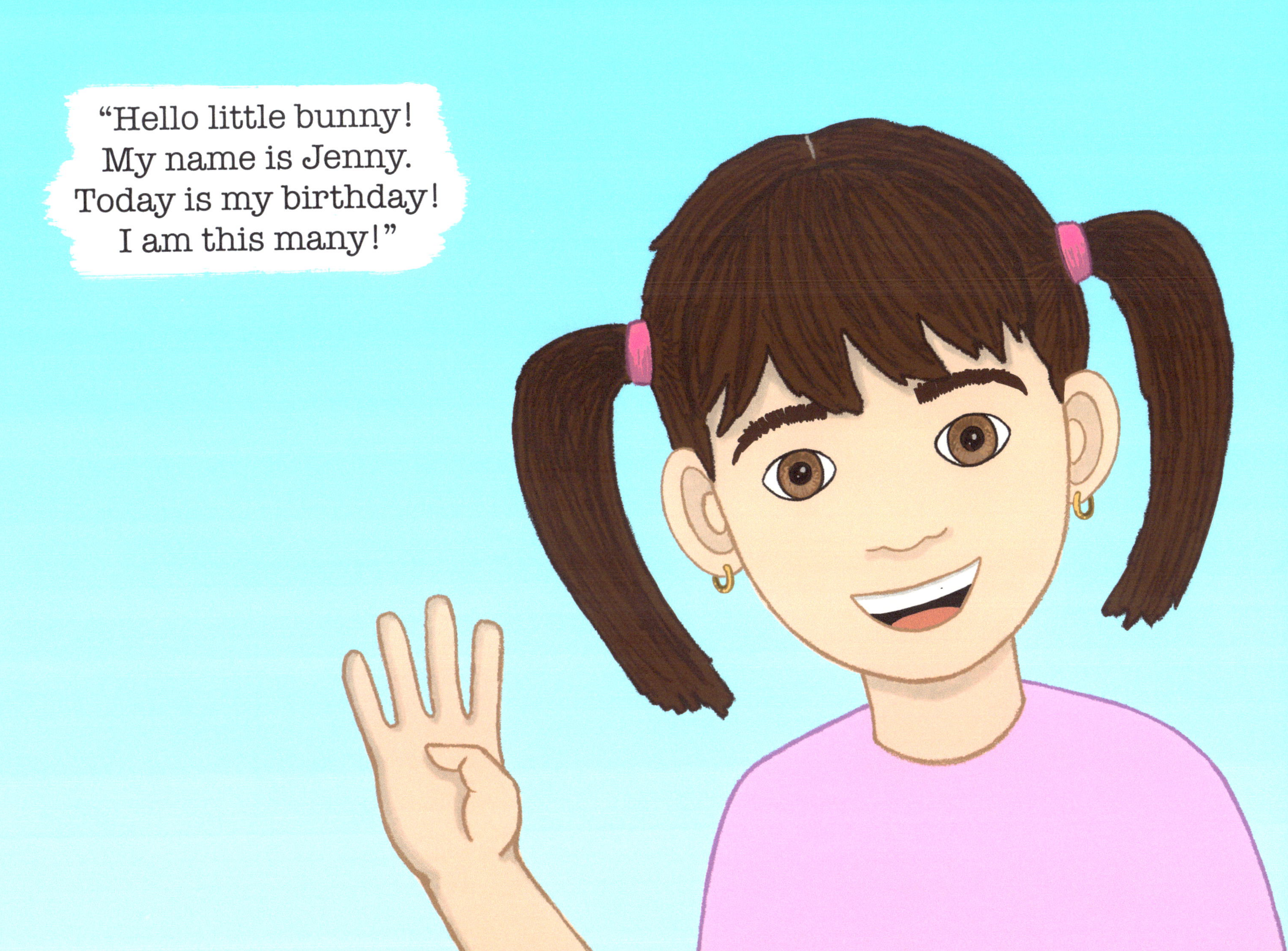

"Hello little bunny!
My name is Jenny.
Today is my birthday!
I am this many!"

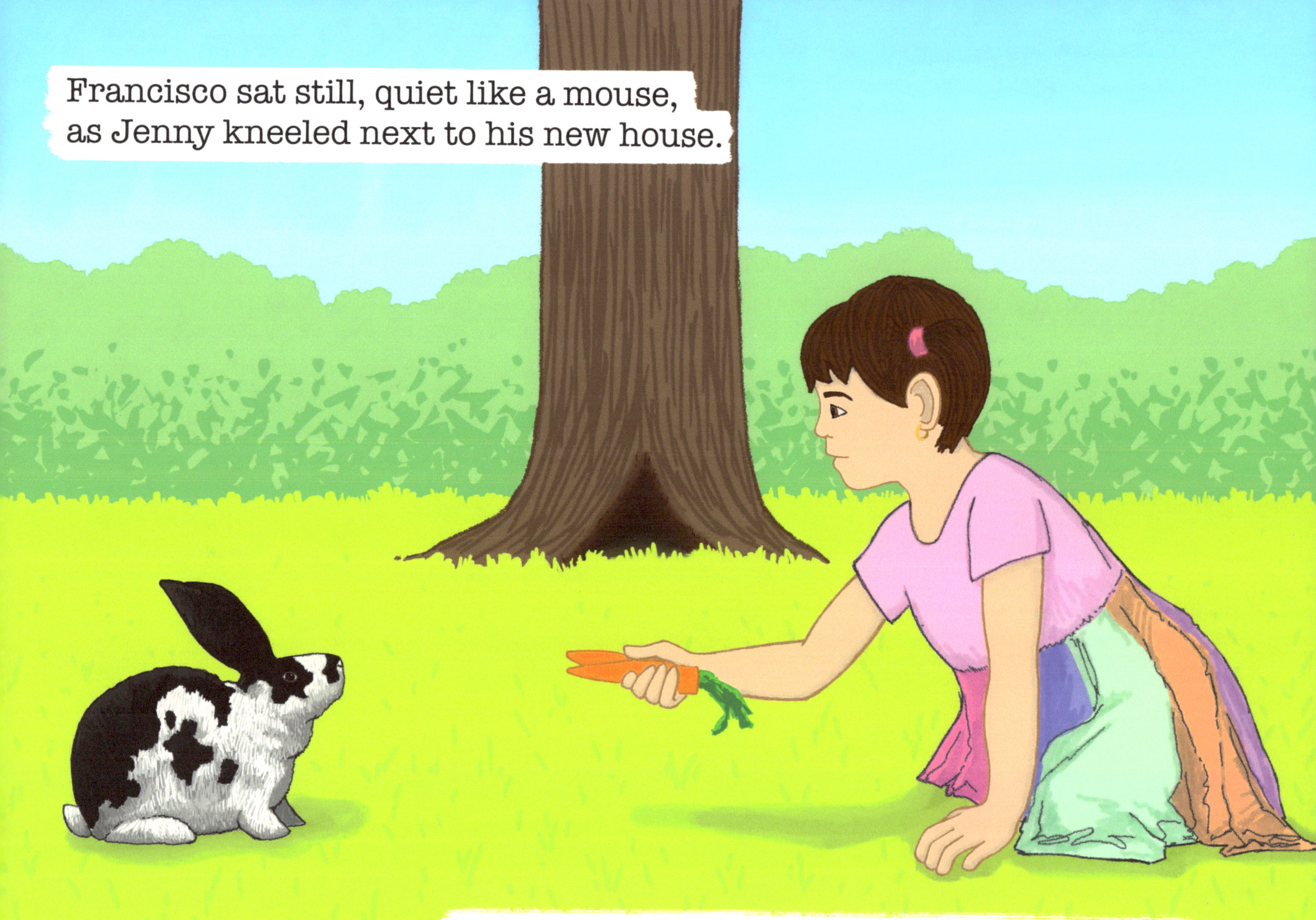

Francisco sat still, quiet like a mouse,
as Jenny kneeled next to his new house.

"Don't be scared little bunny. I won't hurt you.
Would you like a carrot? I have a few."

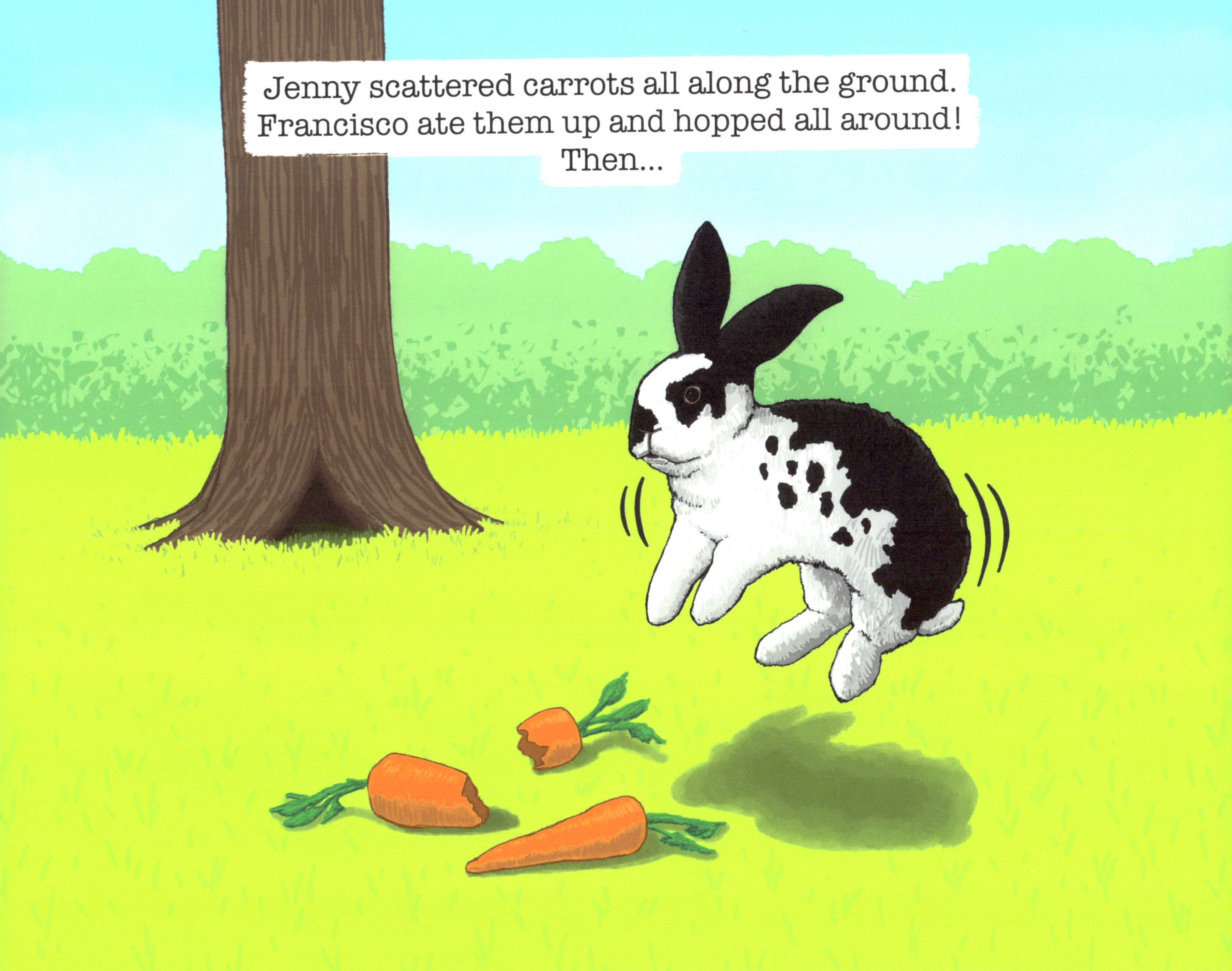

Jenny scattered carrots all along the ground.
Francisco ate them up and hopped all around!
Then...

...they nibbled on cupcakes!

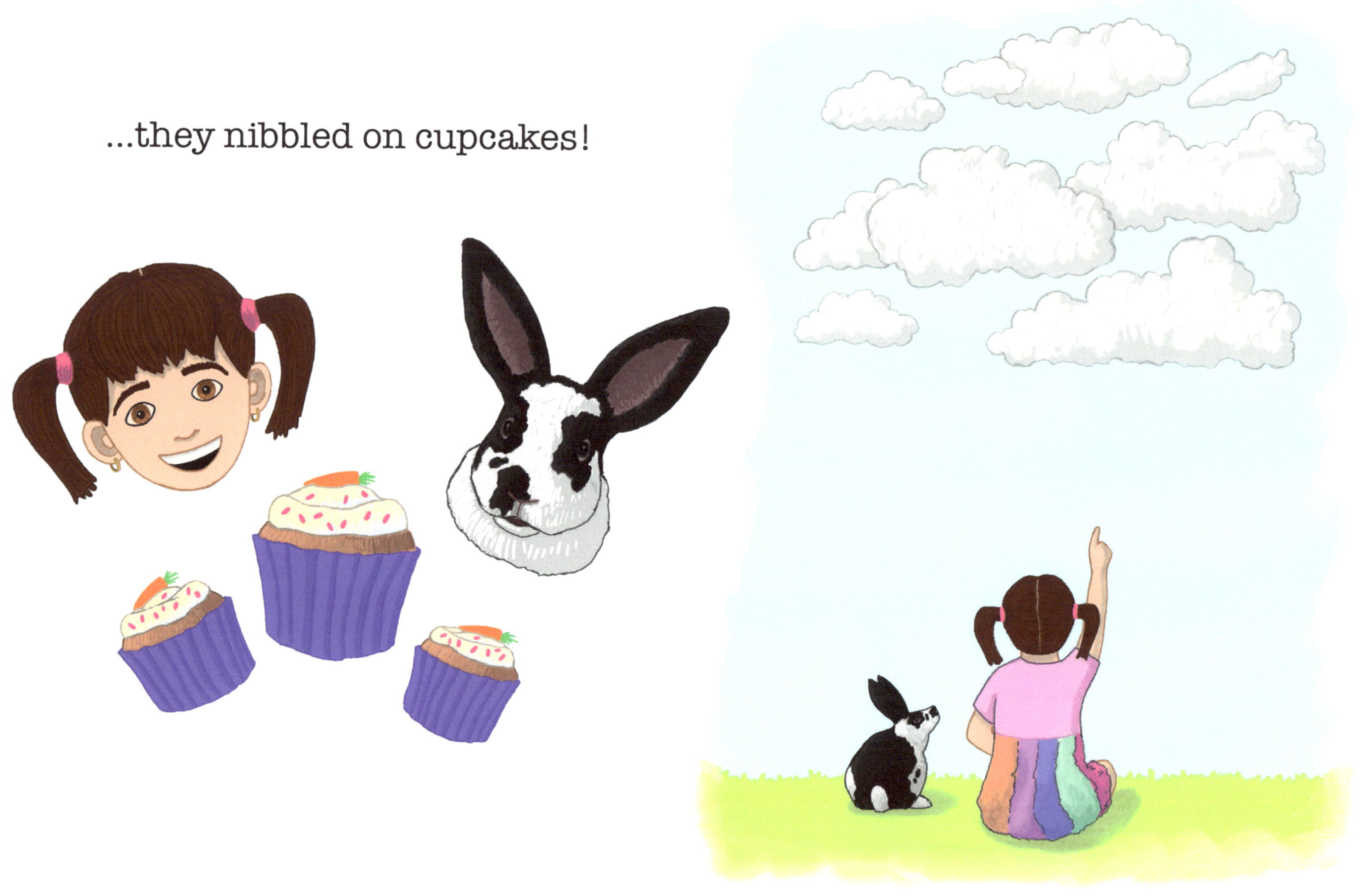

They counted the clouds!

They played hide and seek...

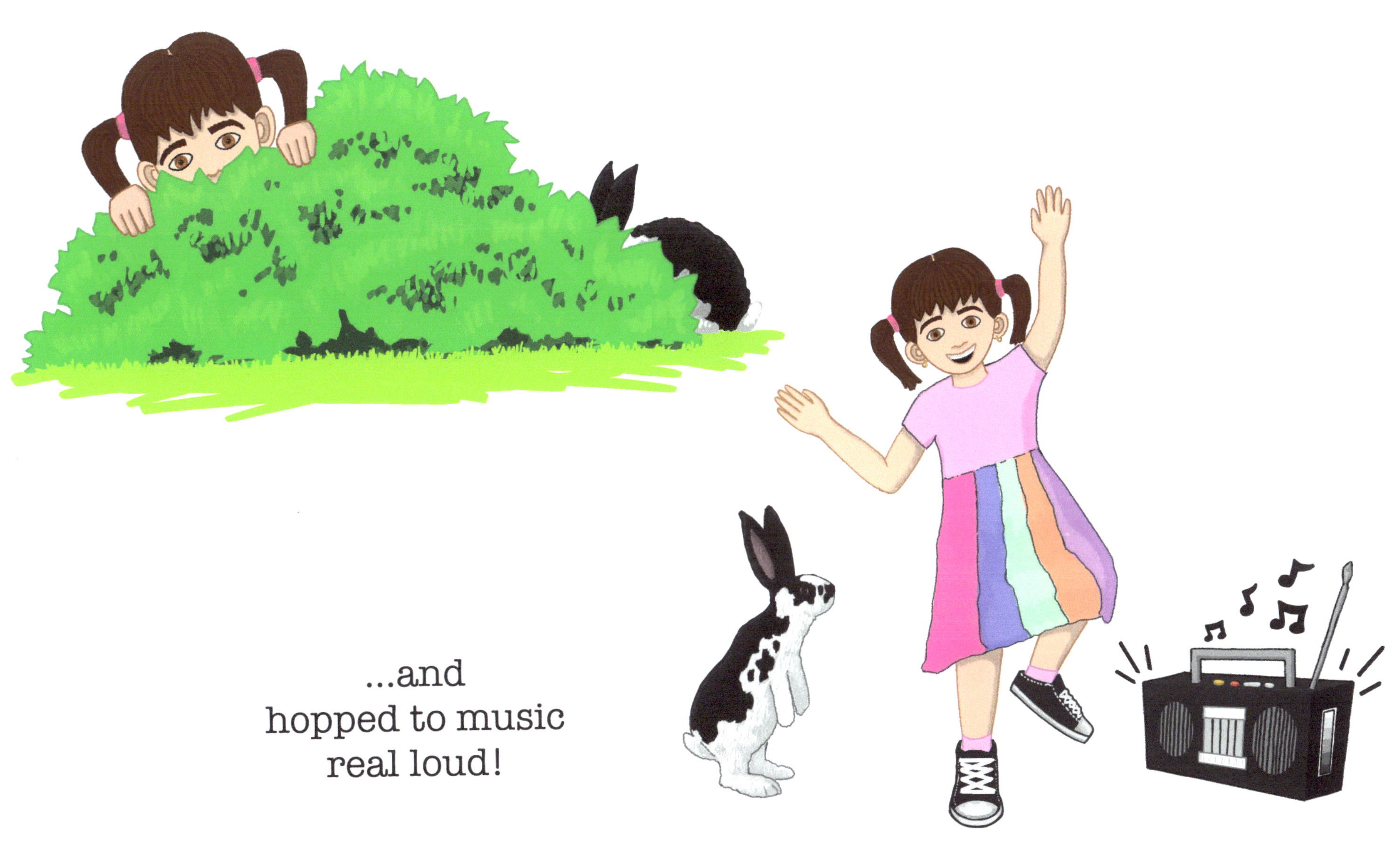

...and
hopped to music
real loud!

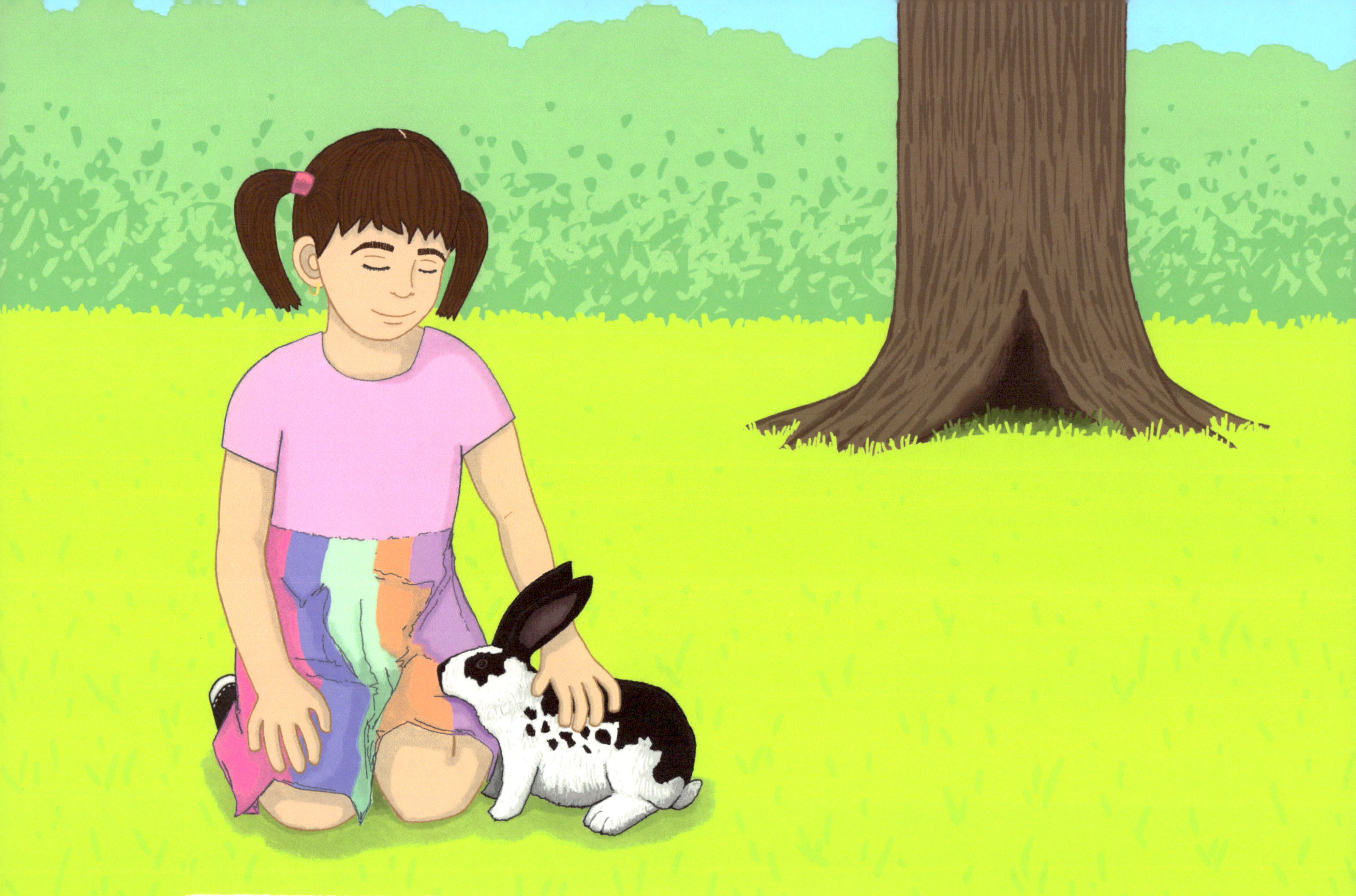

Francisco nuzzled Jenny to let her know,
he was thankful for her kindness, and liked the burrow.

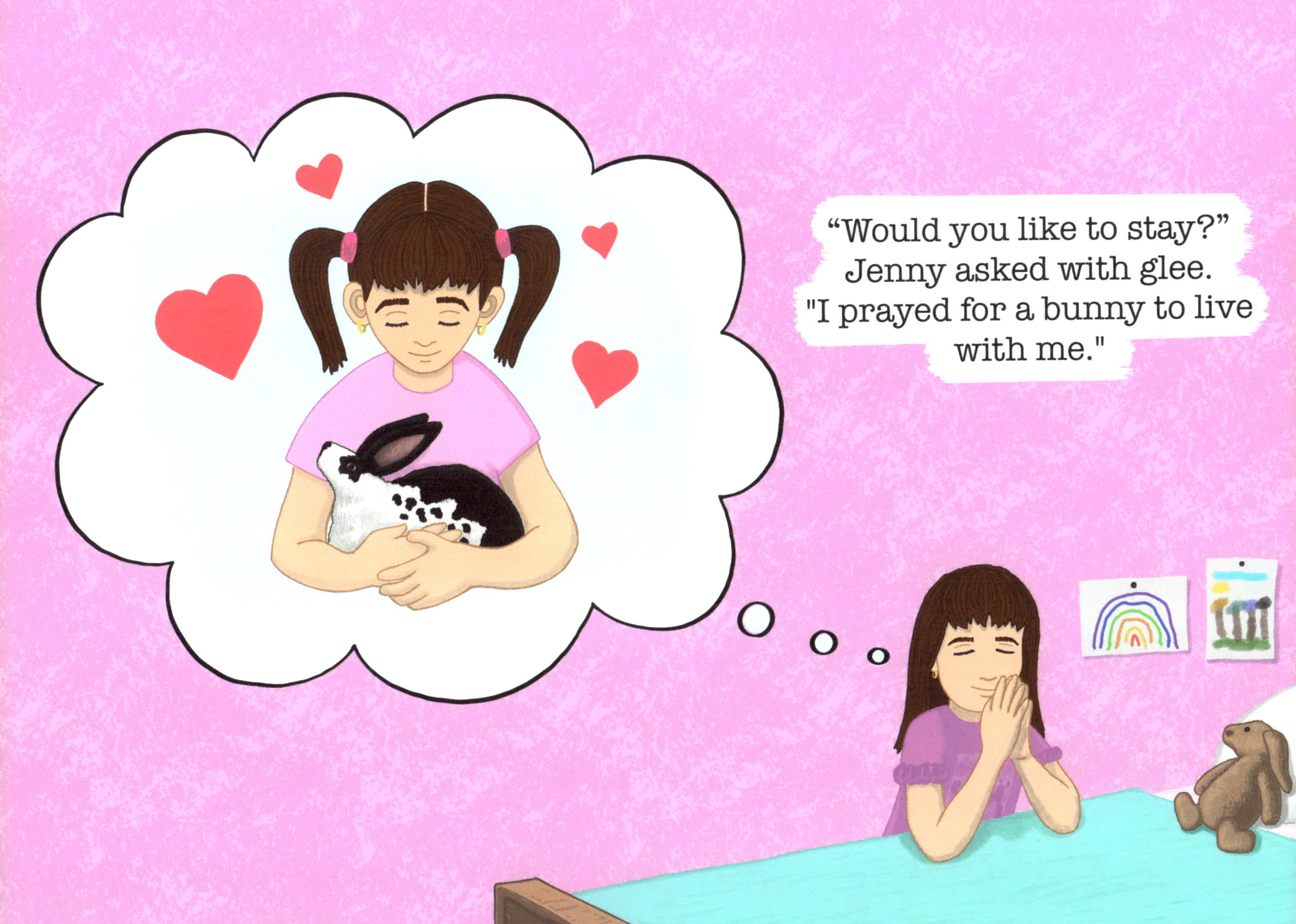

"Would you like to stay?"
Jenny asked with glee.
"I prayed for a bunny to live
with me."

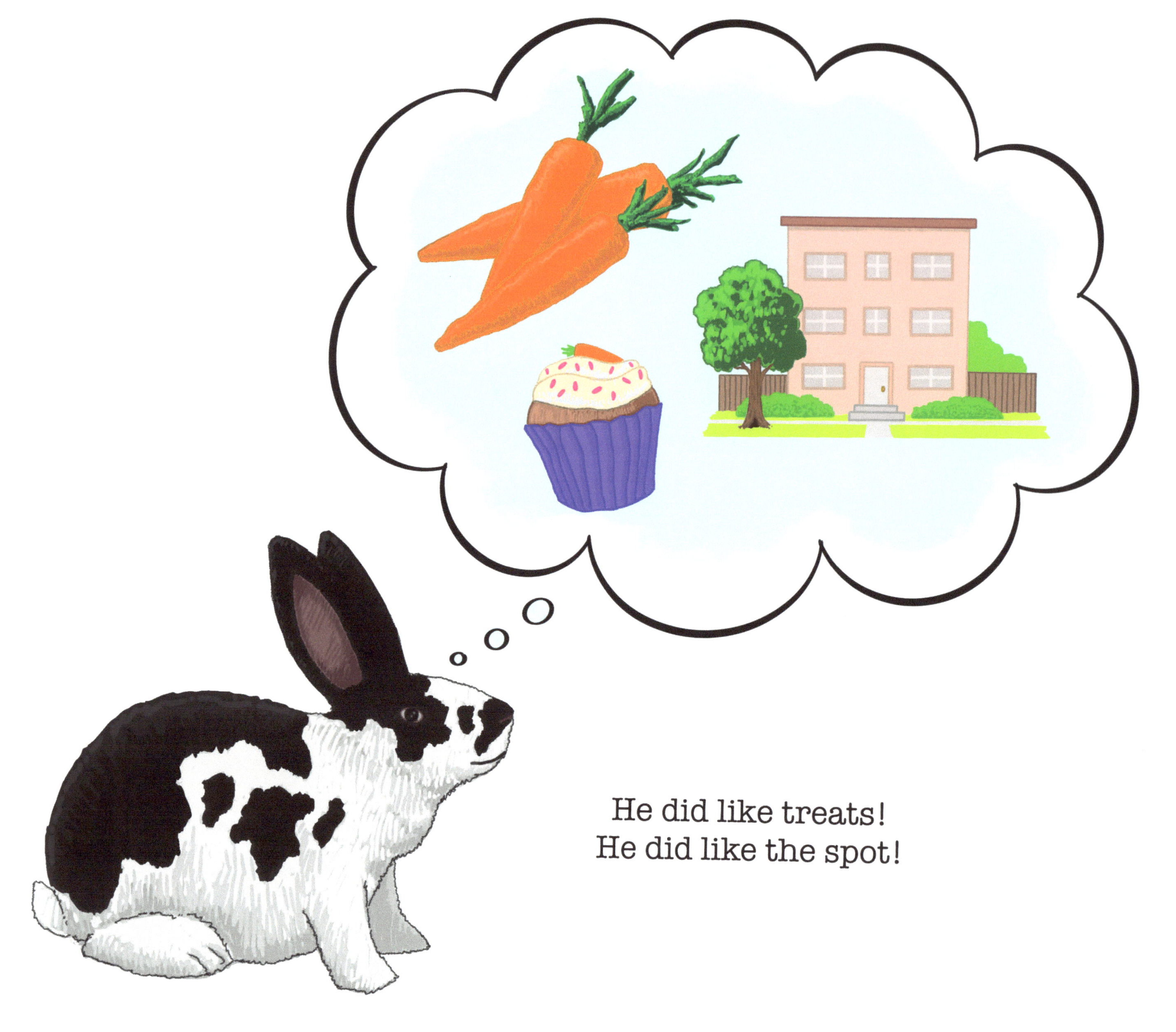

He did like treats!
He did like the spot!

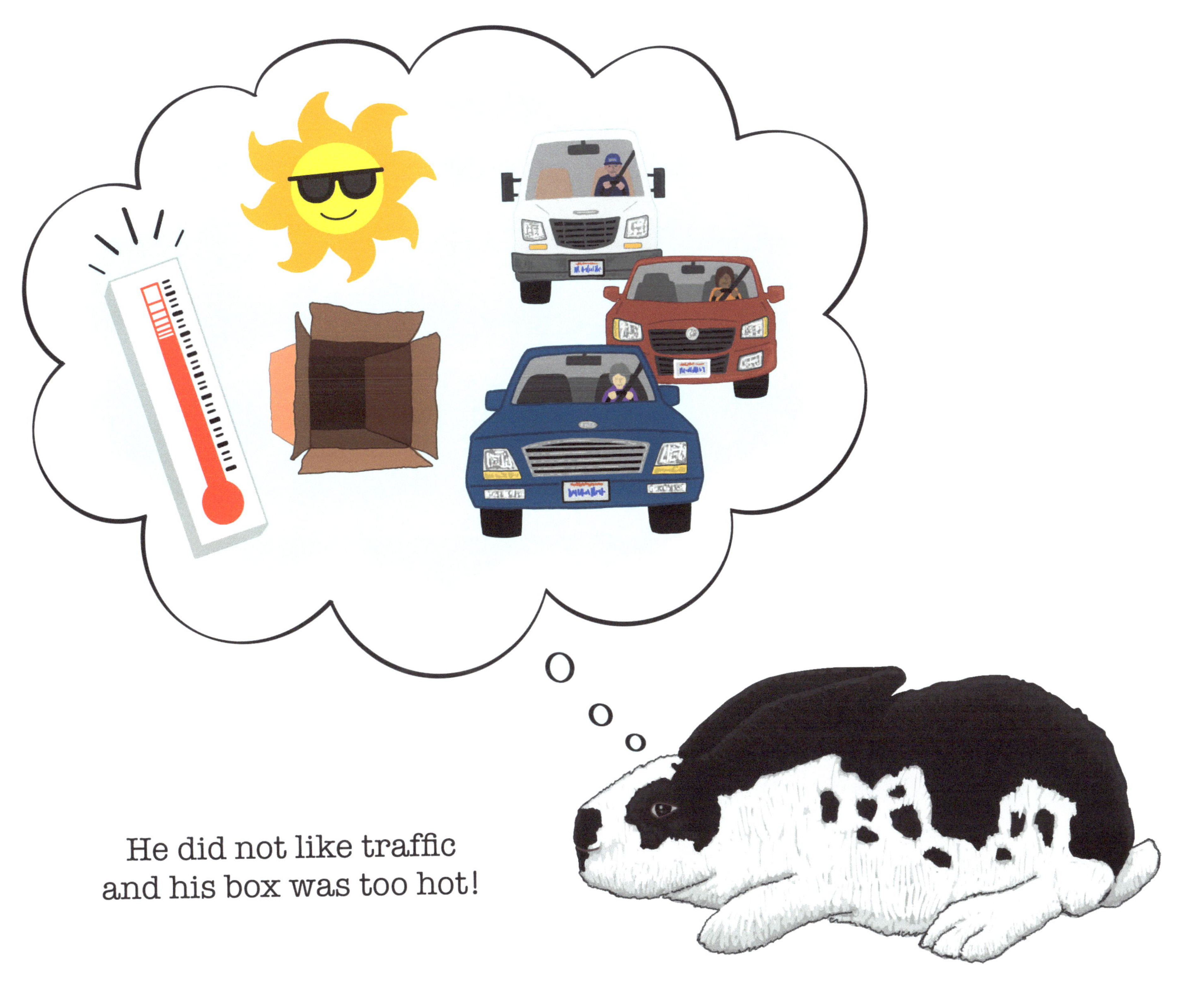

He did not like traffic
and his box was too hot!

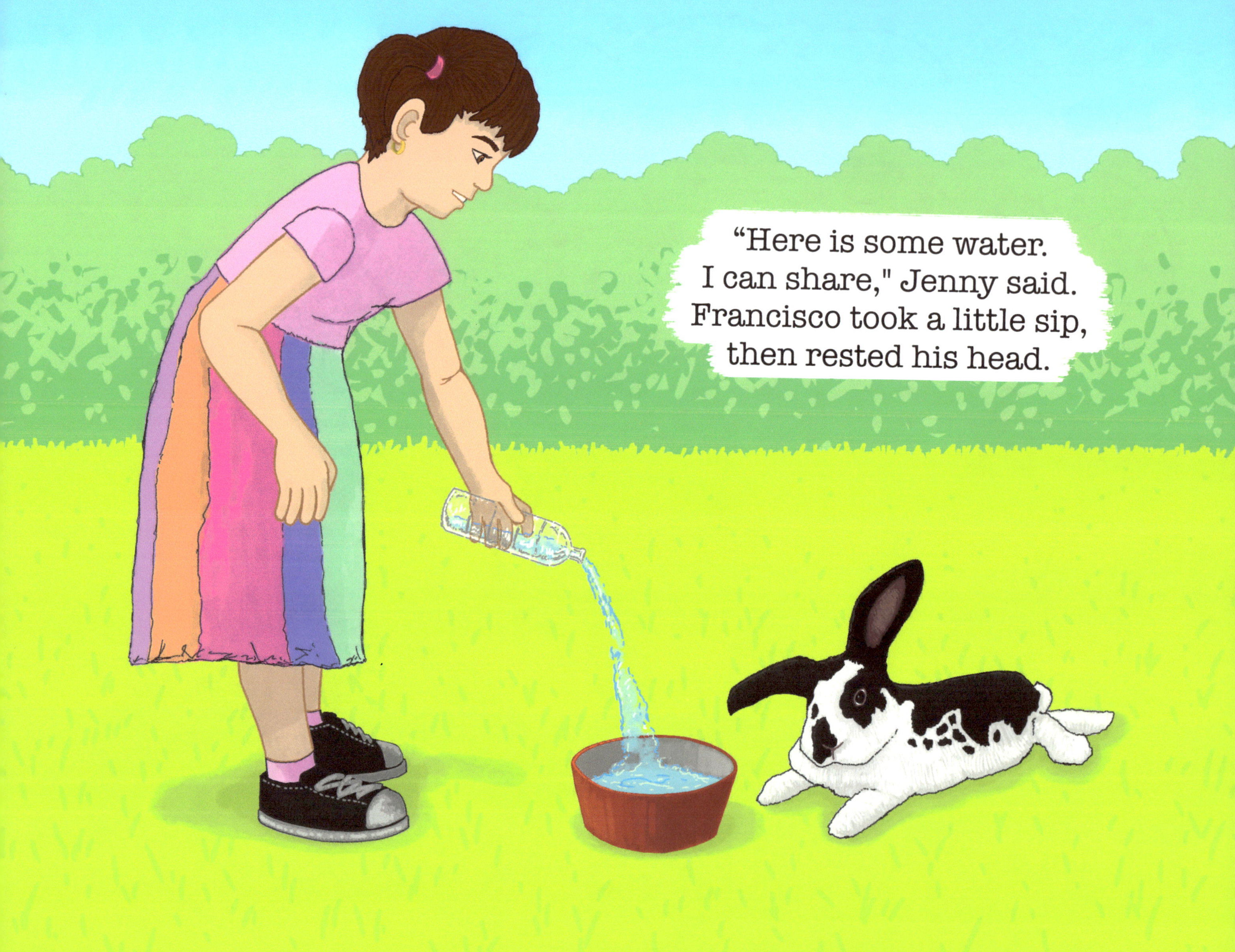

"Here is some water.
I can share," Jenny said.
Francisco took a little sip,
then rested his head.

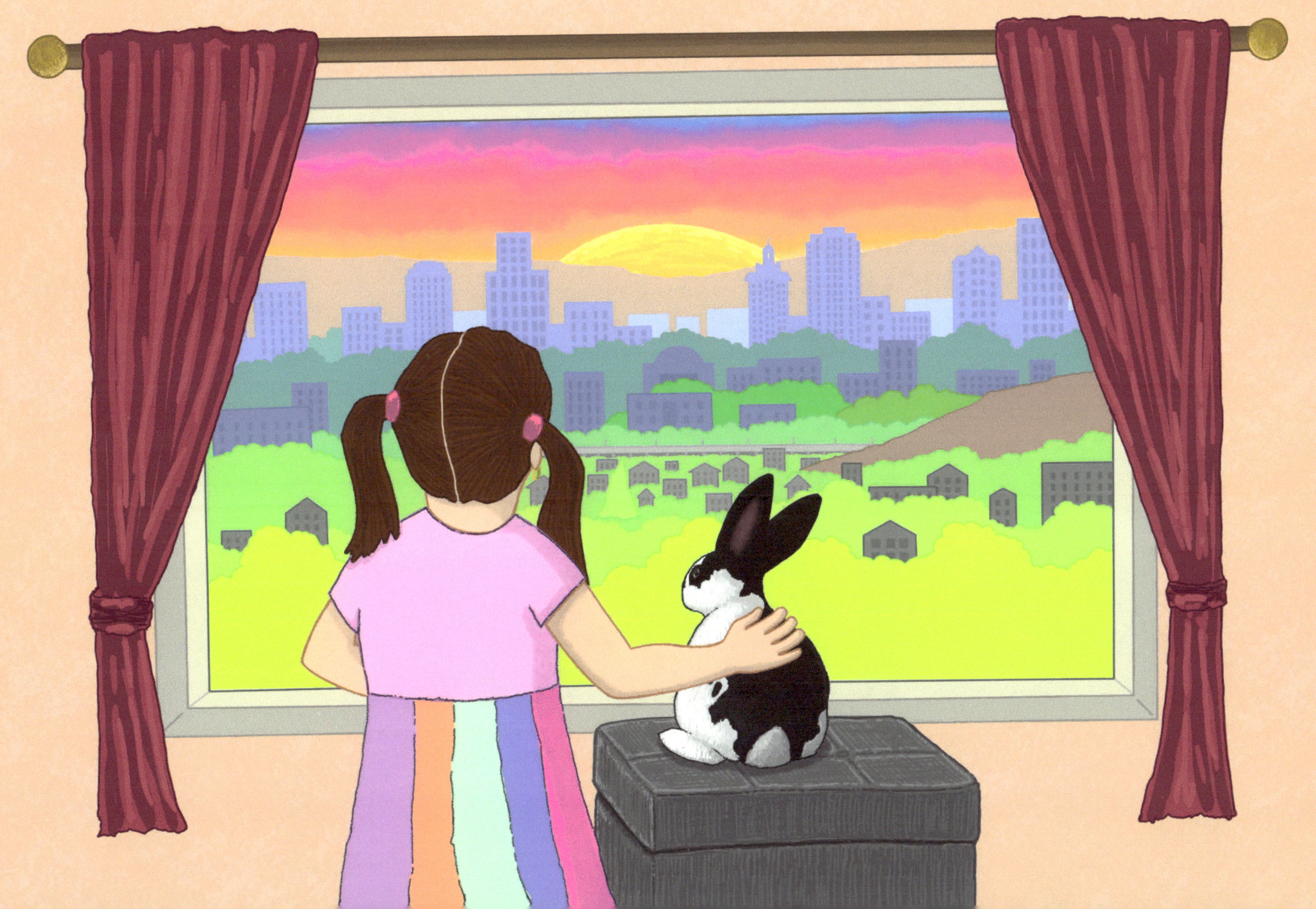
As the sun set on his adventurous day,
Francisco the bunny decided to stay.

BASED ON A TRUE STORY

Francisco the bunny, was found on April 2005 scampering around South 11th Street in downtown San Jose, California. Worried someone might be looking for a lost rabbit, Jenny and Tony brought Francisco to the San Jose Animal Care Center. The center notified Jenny that although Francisco's original owners were located, they didn't want him anymore, choosing to abandon Francisco instead of a safe surrender. Determined to avoid the possibility of Francisco being euthanized, Jenny and Tony adopted Francisco! To learn more about the rabbit rescue organizations the author and illustrator support, please visit franciscothebunny.com

ACKNOWLEDGEMENTS

Special thanks to our editorial team (Beth, Harold, Ginger, Casey, Debbie & Katie) for generously sharing your expertise and time with us to make this book the best it could be. To our launch team, thank you for genuinely supporting our little book even when it was just scribbles in a composition notebook and sketches shared to social media. Lastly, a teary eyed, heartfelt "thank you" to the little bunny who started it all.

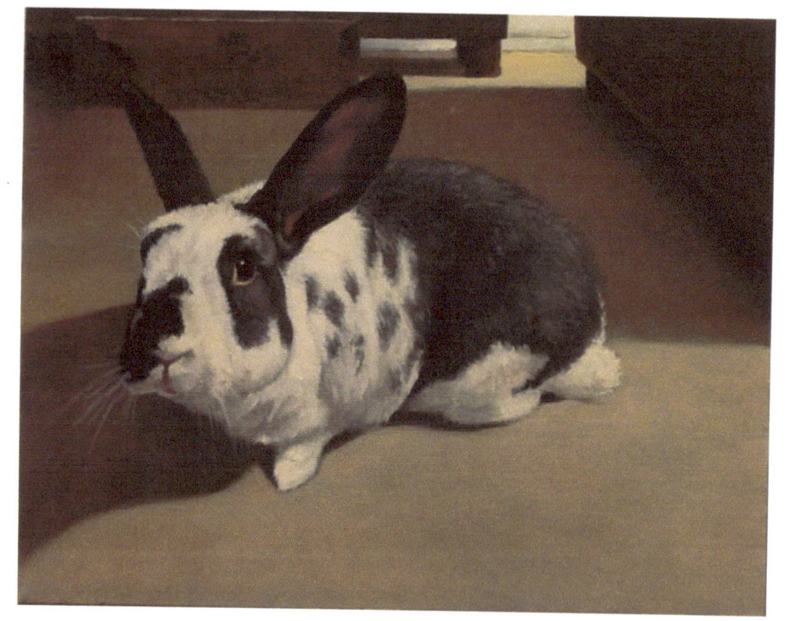

Francisco the bunny
April 2005 - December 2013

ABOUT THE AUTHOR

Jenny Baran, author of Francisco the Bunny, earned her BS in Public Relations from San Jose State University and MA in Pastoral Ministries from Holy Names University. Born in San Francisco, California, Jenny has crafted career paths in children's dance instruction and social work simultaneously. Her dance training from Schumacher's School of Dance, Notre Dame De Namur University's School of Theater and tap master Sam Weber's improvisation classes, led Jenny to teaching children's dance classes for several award-winning studios across the San Francisco Bay Area and Sacramento. Jenny has helped hundreds of parents and children through her past case management work with Placer County Office of Education, San Jose State University Enrollment Services, and other educational institutions in Northern California.

ABOUT THE ILLUSTRATOR

Tony Baran, illustrator of Francisco the Bunny, earned his BA in Pictorial Arts from San Jose State University. Born in Santa Barbara, California, Tony recently retired from a 14 year long career as a Sign Artist for Trader Joe's to meet demand for his pet portraits, landscape paintings and chalk signs through Tony Baran Art. His paintings have been exhibited at the Sanchez Art Center 50/50 Show, Silicon Valley Open Studios, The Art Box Project and the South San Francisco Cultural Art Commission's General Art Show, where he was awarded 1st Place for his landscape painting titled "Hiking the PG&E Trail". Recently, Tony received the "Talent Prize Award" for his pet portrait of the real Francisco the Bunny in the Art Show International Gallery - 2022 International Juried Art Competition.

franciscothebunny.com

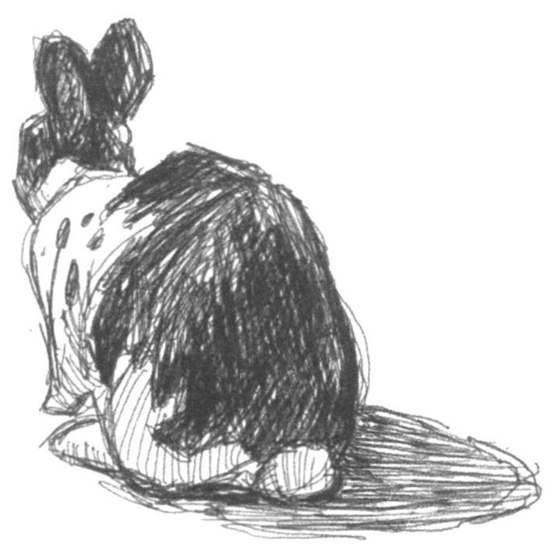